S0-BJJ-830

Traditional Italian Recipes

4

© copyright: 1999, maria pacini fazzi editore

via dell'Angelo Custode, 33 - 55100 Lucca
tel 0583 440188 - fax 0583 464656
www.pacinifazzi.it - mpf@pacinifazzi.it

Proprietà letteraria riservata
Printed in Italy

Drawings by: Paolo Masciullo

ISBN 88-7246-215-0

Traditional recipes from Florence

by

Carla Geri Camporesi

Drawings by

Paolo Masciullo

maria pacini fazzi editore

Liquid Measures Conversion Chart

Fluid Ounces	U.S. Measures	Milliliters
	1 tps	5
1/4	2 tps	7
1/2	1 tbs	15
1	2 tbs	23
2	¼ cup	56
6	¾ cup	170
8	1 cup or ½ pint	225
9		250 – ¼ liter
18	2 ½ cups	500 – ½ liter
36	4 ½ cups	1000 - 1 liter
72	9 cups	2000 – 2 liter

Solid Measures Conversion Chart

Ounces	Pounds	Grams	Kilos
1		28	
3 ½		100	
4	1/4	112	
5		140	
8	1/2	225	
9		250	¼
12	3/4	340	
16	1	450	
18		500	½
20	1 ¼	560	
24	1 ½	675	
27		750	¾
28	1 ¾	780	
32	2	900	
36	2 ¼	1000	1

All conversions are approximate.
They have been rounded off to the nearest convenient measure

Classwork: Tuscan recipes, strictly from Florence

Recipes of strictly Tuscan origin are for those traditional dishes where olive oil, bread-based soups, spit-roasted meat and cannellini are never missing: simple, genuine dishes smacking of the fields, mountains and woods. For the people of Tuscany, authenticity is an inborn requirement, never disregarded, whatever the circumstances. This leads to exhaustive searches for fresh local produce, prompted by an unassuming thrift.

I refer here to dishes, as they have been cooked in the family, over generations. From the very first moment, great care is taken over their preparation, succeeded by the patience to follow and supervise cooking, for long periods, if necessary. Sometimes imagination and the necessity to substitute for a missing ingredient result in a new combination.

Dishes arrive at the table, simply presented, without manipulation, preceded by an appetising smell, permeating the house, of herbs, garlic, oil and excellent wine.

There are some immediate queries regarding cookery of strictly Florentine origin: is this cookery from the city of Florence? from the provinces? or from border communities? The same recipes vary from house to house, and perhaps mother and daughter deal with the same dish in a different way. This is part of the Tuscan character-controversial, never in agreement, and at the same time, never boring or repetitious.

Inventive, and aware of having contributed to the spread of Tuscan cookery outside the region, the people of Florence defend their basic dishes. These are simple, almost to the point of being banal, occasionally permitting last minute flashes of inspiration which leave no lasting traces.

Leaving out inevitable modifications prompted by the individual skill of various cooks (of high standing or housewives at home), for this little collection of recipes, I have chosen only the more usual ones: "cookery recipes, strictly from Florence".

(Unless otherwise stated, all amounts are for six people)

APPETIZERS

SAUCES, and SEASONINGS

"Crostini neri" (with liver)

200 g (8 oz) chicken liver, 200 g (8 oz) veal spleen, 30 g (1 oz) butter, 1 small onion, 50 g (2 oz) anchovy fillet, 50 g (2 oz) capers, 1 glass dry white wine, stock, extra virgin olive oil, salt and pepper 300 g (12 oz) home made bread.

Chop the onion finely, and soften it gently in a little extra virgin olive oil and butter. Meanwhile, clean and prepare the liver being careful to eliminate all traces of gall bladder, which is extremely bitter. Use the blunt edge of a knife to remove the skin of the spleen. Add spleen and chicken livers, finely chopped, to the fried onions, and continue cooking on a moderate heat for half an hour, basting occasionally with the white wine. Mince together the capers and boned anchovy fillets, add these to the mixture with a very little stock, season with salt and pepper, and put it all back on the stove for a few minutes. Toast some slices of home made bread, dip them quickly into the stock, and spread with the liver paste.

"Panzanella" (Soaked bread dish)

300 g (12 oz) stale home-made bread, 3 small fresh onions. 3 ripe tomatoes, 1 cucumber, basil, vinegar, extra virgin olive oil, salt

Cut the bread into thin slices and soak them in cold water for half an hour, then squeeze all the water out by hand. Crumble the bread and put it into a soup tureen. Cut up the tomatoes and add them to the breadcrumbs, first removing the seeds. Cut the cucumber and peeled onion into thin slices and add these to the bread together with five or six washed basil leaves, oil and salt. Mix it all carefully. Just before serving, add the vinegar plus some more oil, and salt if necessary.

"Crostoni" with red cabbage

A recipe to use when the olives are just being harvested, to taste the new oil

500 g (1 lb 2 oz) red cabbage, 1 stock cube, 1 garlic clove, extra virgin olive oil. home made bread, salt and pepper

Boil the red cabbage for about an hour in plenty of lightly salted water containing the stock cube. Meanwhile, toast six medium-size slices of household bread (usually called dark bread). Rub a little garlic on to the slices, quickly dip them into the cabbage cooking water, and arrange them on a dish. As soon as the cabbage is cooked, chop it up and spread it over the slices of toast which are ready on the dish. Salt and pepper lightly, and sprinkle with oil.

"Crostoni" with cannellini beans

The only difference from the preceding recipe is that beans are substituted for cabbage

Soak 200 g (8 oz) of cannellini beans for at least 12 hours, then boil them in salted water containing 2 tablespoonfuls of oil, a clove of garlic and two bay leaves or two sage leaves. Drain off the water and distribute the beans on the slices of toast. Sprinkle with plenty of extra virgin olive oil, and add freshly milled black pepper to taste.

Fried sage

24 large sage leaves, 1 egg, 100 g (4 oz) flour, a few anchovies, extra virgin olive oil, salt

Make a very runny batter with the flour, egg, 1 tablespoonful of oil, a pinch of salt and water if necessary. Clean and bone the anchovies, Wash them well to remove all traces of salt. Take two sage leaves at a time, insert a piece of anchovy and press well between the palm of the hand. Dip the prepared leaves in the batter and fry them in very hot, but not boiling oil. Put the fried leaves on absorbent kitchen paper to soak up any excess frying oil, and serve hot.

"Crescentine salate" (Savoury shapes)

500 g (1 lb 2 oz) flour, 20 g (1 oz) butter or lard, 1 scant tbsp baking powder, stock, salt, extra virgin olive oil

Put the flour, baking powder, a pinch of salt and the butter or lard on to a pastry board and mix the ingredients together, adding enough

stock to make a soft, well kneaded dough.
Roll this out into a square of about 20 cm.
Fold it in four and roll it out again. repeat this
procedure four or five times, then roll the
dough out to a thickness of about 5 mm, and
cut it into diamond shapes. Put oil or lard, or
a mixture of the two, into a frying pan and
heat well. the fat must be boiling. Fry the
little shapes a few at a time. Turn them over
as soon as one side starts to brown, being
careful not to pierce them. Put the shapes on
to a dish lined with absorbent paper, salt
lightly, and serve hot.

"Roventini" (Little black-pudding style pancakes)

*500 g (1 lb 2 oz) pig's blood, 100 g (4 oz) flour, 50 g
(2 oz) pine nuts, 50 g (2 oz) raisins, 1 litre (2 pints)
stock, lard, spices, salt and pepper, parmesan*

To prepare the stock put a small piece of pig's
head into cold, lightly salted water, together
with herbs and vegetables (celery, carrot,
spring onion, parsley and bay leaves). Heat
up and boil for about an hour, then strain it.
Add the stock to the liquid pig's blood, and
then add the flour, salt, pepper, a pinch of
powdered spice, the raisins and pine nuts. Stir
and mix thoroughly so that there are no

lumps. Heat up a non-stick frying pan greased with lard. Drop in two tablespoonfuls of the mixture and cook the pancakes on both sides. Continue until all the mixture is used up. Roll up the little pancakes, sprinkle them with grated parmesan and serve very hot.

Polenta and mushroom crostini

300 g (10 oz) small porcini-type mushrooms (ceps), 2 cloves garlic, 1 sprig calamint, extra virgin olive oil, salt and pepper, maize meal polenta

Clean the mushrooms carefully, removing the earth from the stalks and lightly scraping the caps. Rinse them quickly in water and dry well. Take a small pan and put in it three tablespoonfuls of oil, 2 cloves of garlic, a sprig of calamint, the finely chopped mushrooms, salt and pepper. Cover, and cook over a moderate heat for 20 minutes, then take off the saucepan lid and let the contents thicken. Cut the polenta into little rectangles (about 7/8 cm by 5/6 cm). and fry them in olive oil, or else grill them. Dress the polenta with mushroom sauce, and serve hot.

SAUCES AND SEASONINGS

Meat sauce

400 g (14 oz) beef, 400 g (16 oz) very ripe tomatoes (or else a tin of peeled tomatoes "pelati"), 20 g (1 oz) dried mushrooms, 1 onion, 1 carrot, 1 stick of celery, a few basil leaves, extra virgin olive oil. 1 glass red wine, a little stock, salt and pepper

Wash and finely chop the carrot, celery, onion and basil. Put these into a casserole to brown (possibly a terracotta earthenware one), together with salt, pepper, oil and the meat cut into pieces. Leave the casserole uncovered, and when the meat has browned, pour on the wine, let it evaporate and add the peeled and finely chopped tomatoes. Continue cooking slowly for another 15 minutes, stirring now and then. Soften the mushrooms in lukewarm water. When the meat is done, take it out of the casserole and mince it, together with the mushrooms. Put it all back into the casserole, add the mushrooms soaking water, and continue cooking uncovered for a further half an hour on a moderate heat.

Vegetarian sauce

400 g (14 oz) ripe tomatoes, celery, onion, carrot, 1 garlic clove, parsley, 2 zucchini (courgettes), 1 artichoke, asparagus tips, oregano, thyme, marjoram, basil, sage, bay leaves, salt and pepper, 1 stock cube, extra virgin olive oil

Chop together finely and thoroughly the onion, garlic, celery, carrot, parsley, basil and sage. Put these to brown in three tablespoonfuls of oil, using an earthenware casserole. Add small leaves of thyme, marjoram and oregano, plus two whole bay leaves, the peeled chopped tomatoes, the zucchini (courgettes), cut into rounds, the asparagus tips and the chopped artichoke. Cook it all for a good hour, adding a small amount of stock cautiously as necessary.

Sour sauce

2 bunches of sour white grapes, 1 small onion, 1 small garlic clove, 20 nut kernels, 20 almonds, parsley, a small amount of soft bread, sugar, salt and pepper

Scald the shelled nuts and almonds in boiling water, then drain and peel them. Carefully pound together in a mortar the grapes, the onion, the previously chopped garlic, a handful of small parsley leaves, three or four tablespoonfuls of soft bread, a teaspoonful of sugar, the almonds, nut kernels, salt and pepper, afterwards rubbing it all through a sieve. Put the puree in a small pan to heat it up without letting it boil. Dilute if necessary with a little stock. Serve in a sauce dish as a seasoning for meat.

FIRST COURSES

Polenta dumplings

500 g (1 pound) yellow maize meal, 300 g (12 oz) stewing pork or sausage chunks, 100 g (4 oz) dried mushrooms, 1 small onion, tomato puree, extra virgin olive oil, 1 stock cube, parmesan, butter, salt

Soften the mushrooms in lukewarm water. Take an earthenware casserole, and put in two tablespoonfuls of oil, a little butter, plus a thinly sliced onion, and fry gently. Add the pork or sausage chunks. As soon as the meat has turned colour, pour in a glassful of stock blended with two tablespoonfuls of tomato puree. Add the well squeezed mushrooms, season with salt, and mix well. Cover, and cook for one and a half hours. Separately, put two litres of salted water in a pan (preferably a large copper one). When the water starts to boil, add the maize meal in a steady stream (a pioggia), and cook it for about 45 minutes, stirring continually to avoid lumps. Five minutes before taking it off the heat, add 50 g (1 3/4 oz) of butter and six tablespoonfuls of grated parmesan cheese. The polenta will be extremely soft. Tip it out on to a suitable board, and using a spoon, transfer it into a large bowl, dressing it in layers with the prepared stew.

Stuffed pasta (agnolotti) Tuscan style

for the pasta: 450 g (1 lb) white flour, 4 eggs

for filling: 250 g (10 oz) veal, 100 g (4 oz)brains, 100 g (4 oz) mortadella sausage, parmesan cheese, 2 eggs, stock, soft bread, extra virgin olive oil, nutmeg, salt

for the dressing: butter and parmesan cheese

Soak the soft bread in lukewarm water. Take a small pan, put in three tablespoonfuls of olive oil, cut the veal into pieces and brown it in the oil. Pour in a little stock and bring it slowly to cooking temperature. When the veal is well done, mince it finely and put it in a bowl. Under cold running water remove the membranes from the brains, clean away all traces of blood, cut into small pieces and add to the veal with the previously squeezed out bread, the minced mortadella, four tablespoonfuls of grated parmesan, two eggs and a pinch of nutmeg. Blend it all well together. To prepare the pasta, put the flour and eggs on to a pastry board, adding two tablespoonfuls of milk if necessary. Work it all well together, and roll it out thinly. Put the filling in little mounds three centimetres apart, starting three or four centimetres from the edge. Fold the free side of the pastry on top of the little mounds. Use a finger to press it down all around, and cut out with a suitable notched pastry wheel. Cook the "agnolotti" for a few minutes in plenty of salted water. Serve with a dressing of butter and grated parmesan, or else with sauce.

Tuscan ravioli

2 kg (4 1/2 pounds) spinach, 400 g (16 oz) ricotta (soft curd cheese), 3 eggs, a little flour, 100 g (4 oz) butter, parmesan cheese, nutmeg, salt

Wash the spinach carefully removing any yellow or damaged leaves. Boil the spinach in a covered pan with just the water which still clings to the leaves, salting lightly. When it is cooked, drain, chop finely and leave to cool. Put the ricotta into a bowl and mix it with three whole eggs, a pinch of salt and nutmeg and two generous handfuls of parmesan, Add the chopped spinach to this mixture and blend well. Make little oval-shaped rissoles, flour them lightly and line them up on a clean linen cloth. Heat up a large pan of lightly salted water, and when it boils drop in a few ravioli at a time. Take them out of the water with a perforated spoon as soon as they rise to the surface, and put them on a wide serving dish. Dress the ravioli with melted (not fried) butter, and plenty of grated parmesan. Serve very hot.

Penne pasta from the pan

400 g (16 oz) pasta "penne" type, 200 g (8 oz) lean red minced meat, 100 g (4 oz) bacon, 2 chicken livers, 2 carrots, 1 stick of celery, 1 small onion, a little parsley, 400 g (16 oz) peeled tomatoes, 30 g (1 oz) butter, extra virgin olive oil, 1 glass red wine, salt and pepper

Mix together the very finely chopped flavouring herbs and vegetables and brown gently in four tablespoonfuls of oil and 30 g (1 oz) butter. When they are brown, add the meat, bacon and chicken livers, all previously minced, and brown these very gently. Pour in the wine and let it evaporate. Add the peeled tomatoes and cook it all on a moderate heat. Boil the pasta until cooked but not soft ("al dente"), and then drain. Transfer the cooked pasta, together with the sauce into a sufficiently large pan. Sauté it all for two minutes over a good heat and then tip the steaming hot "penne" on to a serving dish.

Minestrone soup

500 g (1 pound) fresh beans, 200 g (8 oz) Savoy cabbage, 2 small bundles of chard, 3 potatoes, 2 sticks of celery, 2 carrots, 3 zucchini (courgettes), 1 large red onion, 1 garlic clove, parsley, 2 ripe tomatoes, a few basil leaves, extra virgin olive oil, 1 stock cube, salt and pepper; 300 g (12 oz) pasta "paternostri" type, or rice, parmesan cheese

Slice the onion thinly and brown it in four tablespoonfuls of oil, adding a spoonful of water to prevent burning. When the onion has turned colour, add the cubed potatoes and brown gently. Add a stock cube and then all the vegetables, cut into cubes, plus the cabbage and chard in thin strips, the beans and the tomatoes. Cover and cook slowly, adding boiling water if the minestrone starts to dry out.

When the vegetables are completely cooked (the carrots will be ready last), add enough boiling water to cook the rice or the pasta. As soon as the water starts to boil again, season with salt and pepper, add the rice or pasta and continue cooking until done.

Serve hot sprinkling a little uncooked extra virgin olive oil on to each plateful of soup. Add grated parmesan to taste.

If dried beans are used (250 g), these should be prepared in advance: put them to soak the previous evening, boil them in lightly salted water and rub all, or some of them through a sieve (a few beans left whole are pleasant). Add to the minestrone when the other vegetables are nearly cooked.

Ribollita

Half a Savoy cabbage, 1 red cabbage, 1 bunch chard, 400 g (16 oz) dried white beans, 2 potatoes, 2 tbsp. tomato puree, 300 g (12 oz) stale home made bread, 2 onions, 1 garlic clove, extra virgin olive oil, salt and pepper

Soak the beans in two litres of cold water and then boil them.

Rub 3/4 of the beans through a sieve, and put the puree back into the cooking water. Put aside the remaining whole beans. Brown the garlic and the chopped onion in 8 tablespoonfuls of oil, and as soon as they have softened, add the two tablespoonfuls of tomato puree diluted with a glass of warm water. Add the very finely chopped carrot and celery, the cabbages and chard, washed and cut into strips, plus the peeled and finely sliced potatoes. Season with salt and pepper, let it cook for a few minutes, and then add the pureed beans. Continue cooking for about an hour. When the vegetables are well done, add the sliced bread and the whole beans previously put aside. Mix well, pour into a soup tureen and serve with a touch of extra virgin olive oil, and with the thinly sliced onion passed round separately.

Red cabbage polenta

1 red cabbage, 150 g (6 oz) maize meal, 2 sticks celery, extra virgin olive oil, parsley, salt

Wash the cabbage, choosing the healthiest looking leaves. Slice it finely together with the celery and parsley, and fry very gently in two tablespoonfuls of oil. Add a litre (2 pints) of hot water, season with salt, cover and cook for 15 minutes. When the cabbage is done, add the maize meal in a steady stream (a pioggia), as for normal polenta, and continue stirring for a further 10-15 minutes. Serve in little bowls with a sprinkling of extra virgin olive oil.

Pappa con il pomodoro (Soaked bread and tomato dish)

300 g (12 oz) stale home made bread, 500 g (1 pound) ripe tomatoes, 2 garlic cloves, 1 litre (2 pints) stock, basil, extra virgin olive oil, salt and pepper

Cut the two garlic cloves in half and brown them in two tablespoonfuls of oil. As soon as they start to turn colour, add the peeled and diced tomatoes, plenty of basil, and salt and pepper to taste. Cook it all for 15 minutes, and then add the boiling stock. When this has reached boiling point again, add the thinly sliced bread and continue cooking for a further 15 minutes, stirring frequently, and then remove from the heat. After an hour, stir it all very energetically so that the bread completely disintegrates. Serve hot or lukewarm, adding a touch of good extra virgin olive oil and a few fresh basil leaves. No cheese.

Pasta with beans

300 g (12 oz) tomato pulp, 1 onion, 1 garlic clove, 1 carrot, 1 celery stick, 300 g (12 oz) dried cannellini beans, basil extra virgin olive oil, salt and pepper, 400 g (16 oz) fresh pasta, wide tagliatelle type

Soak the beans overnight, and then boil them in lightly salted water. Thinly slice the onion and garlic, and soften in three tablespoonfuls of olive oil. When the onion is transparent, add the chopped carrot and celery, the basil leaves and the diced tomato, plus a pinch of salt. Cook for 30-40 minutes, and then add the previously boiled beans. Rub it all through a vegetable sieve, season with salt and pepper, adding boiling water if necessary, When it re-boils, add and cook the pasta. Serve very hot, with a touch of good quality extra virgin olive oil and freshly milled pepper to taste.

Rice and bean soup

*800 g (1 3/4 pound) fresh white beans, 500 g (1 pound)
ripe tomatoes, 50 g (2 oz) bacon, 1 onion, 2 garlic
cloves, 1 small stick of celery, parsley, basil, extra
virgin olive oil, 1 sharp chilli, salt and pepper
400 g (16 oz) rice*

Put the shelled beans in a pan with two litres
(9 cups) of cold water. Bring slowly to
boiling point, cook the beans and add salt
when they are nearly done. Finely chop the
onion, garlic, celery, basil, parsley and a
small piece of red chilli. Fry these gently in
three tablespoonfuls of oil, together with the
bacon, cut into small cubes. When it has all
turned a light golden colour, add the de-
seeded and diced tomatoes. Season with salt
and pepper to taste, and continue cooking
for about 15-20 minutes. Put it all through
a vegetable sieve, and add the beans with
their cooking water. Stir well and continue
cooking for a further 10 minutes, then add
the rice. Serve hot, or lukewarm, without
cheese.

Vegetable risotto

*500 g (1 pound) fresh broad beans, 500 g (1 pound)
ripe tomatoes, 400 g (16 oz) fresh peas, 70 g (3 oz)
bacon, 1 onion, 1 carrot, 1 stick celery, 2 courgettes,*

parsley, basil, extra virgin olive oil, salt and pepper
300 g (12 oz) rice, parmesan

Finely chop the onion, celery, carrot and parsley; cut the bacon into little cubes, and brown all these ingredients in six tablespoonfuls of extra virgin olive oil.

Meanwhile, shell the broad beans and the peas, keeping each separate. When the chopped herbs, vegetables and bacon have turned colour, add the de-seeded tomatoes, the cleaned and diced courgettes and the beans. Season with salt and pepper to taste. Continue cooking for 20 minutes, and then add the peas. Keep a litre of lightly salted boiling water ready on the side. About 10 minutes after adding the peas, add the rice, fry it lightly, and bring everything to cooking temperature, adding constantly boiling water by the ladleful, a little at a time. Before removing the rice from the stove and serving it, stir and blend in plenty of grated parmesan.

"Crespelle" (Florentine savoury stuffed pancakes)

for the pancakes: 100 g (4 oz) flour, 2 eggs, 1 glass milk, 20 g (1 oz) butter, salt for the filling: 500 g (1 pound) spinach, 300 g (12 oz) ricotta, 1 egg, grated parmesan, salt and pepper

for the dressing: 70 g (3 oz) flour, 60 g (2 oz) butter, half litre (2 cups) milk, tomato sauce concentrate, salt and pepper

Wash the spinach repeatedly under running water, removing any damaged leaves. Boil the spinach with just the water remaining on the leaves after washing. When it is cooked, drain, squeeze out well and chop it very finely.

Put the spinach in a bowl, add the ricotta, two tablespoonfuls grated parmesan, a pinch of nutmeg and the egg, seasoning with salt and pepper to taste. Stir the mixture well, using a wooden spoon, so that all the ingredients are well blended.

Make a thin batter with the flour, two eggs, a little salt, a glassful of milk and the melted butter. Let it rest for an hour.

Meanwhile, prepare a fairly thin white sauce. Melt 50 g (2 oz) of butter in a pan, add the flour, cook this for a few seconds and then very gradually pour in the milk, stirring continually to avoid lumps forming. Season with salt and cook the sauce for about 20 minutes. Put a little butter in a small frying pan and make 12 little pancakes with the batter prepared as above.

Use the ricotta mixture as a filling for the

pancakes, rolling them up and arranging them side by side in a greased rectangular ovenproof dish. Cover the stuffed pancakes with the white sauce, and on top of this distribute a few tablespoonfuls of tomato sauce, previously diluted with a little stock. Brown in the oven ("au gratin"), at 180 C, for 15 minutes.

Risotto with meat sauce

100 g (4 oz) minced meat, 2 chicken livers, 2 small onions, 1 carrot, 1 stick of celery, 1 1/2 litres meat stock, extra virgin olive oil, red wine, 8o g (3 oz) butter, tinned tomato concentrate, parmesan cheese
400 g (16 oz) Vialone or Arborio rice

Chop the onion, celery and one carrot. Brown these in half the butter and two tablespoonfuls oil. After this add the minced meat, the very finely chopped livers and 2 tablespoonfuls tomato concentrate diluted with half a cup of hot stock. Cook the sauce, adding a glass of red wine little by little. Season with salt and pepper to taste.
Separately, soften the other onion in two tablespoonfuls of oil and the rest of the butter, and when it is transparent, add the rice and brown it for a few seconds, stirring with a wooden spoon, then add the hot stock. When the rice is two thirds cooked, add the

sauce (reserving some of it to garnish the risotto dish). Just before taking the risotto off the heat, add a good amount of grated parmesan. Put the rice into a suitable serving dish with the rest of the sauce and serve hot.

Pasta and chick peas

300 g (12 oz) flour, 300 g (12 oz) dried chick peas, 2 garlic cloves, 1 sprig rosemary, two tablespoonfuls tomato sauce, extra virgin olive oil, salt and pepper

Soak the chick peas for two days, starting off with lukewarm water, then cook them in plenty of lightly salted water.
Put the flour and a pinch of salt on to a pastry board adding water as needed to make a dough. Work it well and roll it out but not too thinly. Cut it into strips a little bit wider than tagliatelle, and dry on a clean linen cloth.
Brown two garlic cloves and a sprig of rosemary in two tablespoonfuls of oil. Rub half of the chick peas through a sieve and put the resulting puree back into their cooking water together with the strained fried mixture and two tablespoonfuls of tomato sauce. Season with salt and pepper and cook the pasta in the same pan. Serve very hot, with a touch of good quality extra virgin olive oil and, if liked, a little freshly milled pepper.

Tuscan style pasta

*500 g (1 pound) fresh ripe tomatoes, 2 small onions, 1
carrot, 1 stick of celery, basil, extra virgin olive oil, salt
pepper, parmesan*
400 g (16 oz) short pasta or spaghetti

Make some tomato puree by cooking
together the diced, de-seeded and peeled
tomatoes, a sliced onion, the chopped carrot
and celery plus three or four basil leaves.
Cook for 30 minutes in a covered pan, then
pass it all through a vegetable sieve. Brown
the remaining onion in three tablespoonfuls
of oil, possibly adding a tablespoonful of
water to prevent burning, and when the onion
is transparent, add the tomato puree which
has been kept aside. Meanwhile, cook the
pasta in plenty of boiling salted water. When
it is "al dente" (i.e. cooked, but not soft),
dress it with the sauce prepared as above, and
plenty of grated parmesan.

SECOND COURSES

Grilled T-bone steak

700/800 g (1 3/4 pounds) beef cut from the loin to include the fillet and the T-bone steak. The meat must be well hung, for at least 5 or 6 days. Salt and pepper

Prepare the grill so that the charcoal is well lit and red hot without any actual flames. When the grill is really hot, put on the unwashed meat and grill it without turning and without piercing it in any way.(With a T-bone steak, the secret is to cook it very quickly so as to sear and seal in the meat juices).

After five or six minutes, turn the steak over using a spatula, and season with salt and pepper. Grill the other side for a further five minutes, turn the meat over again and season the upper side with salt and pepper. At the end, the meat should be very well done on the outside, but it stays tasty and tender.

Serve hot, without oil, but garnished with slices of lemon.

Roast loin of pork

1500 g (3 pounds) loin of pork on the bone, 1 garlic clove, 1 sprig of rosemary, salt and pepper

Using a sharp pointed knife, draw some of

the meat away from the bone, without detaching it completely.

Thoroughly chop together the rosemary and garlic clove, adding salt and pepper. Make little incisions in the meat and fill these with the chopped herb mixture. Salt the meat, tie it up to keep it in shape, and put it on a large baking tin. Cook in the oven at 180 C for about two hours, turning frequently and basting with the fat which collects in the tin. Sauté some previously boiled cabbage or turnips in the flavoured sauce produced by the meat as it cooks. Serve these vegetables as an accompaniment to the roast which should be carved unto fairly thick slices.

Veal stew with peas

1 kg (2 pounds) stewing veal (cut from the muscle), 1 carrot, 1 celery stick, 1 onion, 2 garlic cloves, a few basil leaves, tomato puree, 1 glass red wine, extra virgin olive oil, salt and pepper

Chop together very finely the onion, garlic, celery and carrot. Brown these gently in three tablespoonfuls of oil. When they have turned colour slightly, add the stewing veal, previously washed, dried and lightly coated with flour. Brown the veal well, then add the wine and cover. As soon as the wine has evaporated, add a glassful of tomato puree, and the basil. Season with salt and pepper, and continue cooking on a very low heat. It should be a long slow process. Add hot water as needed so that the sauce stays thin and there is plenty of it. After about two hours, add the shelled peas and cook these in the stew. It can be served with toasted slices of garlic-flavoured home made bread.

Florentine meat loaf

600 g (1 1/2 pounds) lean veal, 100 g (4 oz) prosciutto, 1 small onion, parsley, 1 stick of celery, 1 carrot, 1 egg, flour, extra virgin olive oil, 1 stock cube, nutmeg, salt and pepper

Clean and mince the meat together with the slice of prosciutto, add the egg, a little salt and pepper, and a pinch of grated nutmeg. Form the mixture into a ball and flour it. Meanwhile, gently brown the finely chopped onion, carrot, parsley and celery in three tablespoonfuls of olive oil. When these have turned colour, put the meat ball into the pan and brown it well on all sides. Add a glass of hot water containing half a dissolved stock cube. Cover and cook slowly, watching to see that the meat does not stick to the pan. Serve hot with its own sauce, and mashed potatoes.

"Peposo" *(Pepper dish)* *(for 8 people)*

2 kg (4 1/2 pounds) muscle of veal taken from the shinbone, 10 cloves garlic, 700 g (1 3/4 pounds) peeled tomatoes, 2 glasses of red wine, 8 coffeespoonfuls freshly milled black pepper, water and salt as needed

Take a deep pan (possibly earthenware), and put in the meat cut into large cubes, the garlic trimmed at the top and bottom, and then cut into little pieces, the tomatoes, salt and pepper.
Cover it all with cold water. Allow to cook slowly for about two hours over a moderate heat, then add the wine and continue cooking for a further hour.

Note: This recipe, by kind permission of Mr Matteini from Impruneta, seems to be the original one which was rediscovered at home of an old family in the country. Obviously, the tomatoes are a later addition because they were unknown in Italy at the time when this brickyard pepper dish was originally prepared.

"Cibreo" *(for 4 people)*

400 g (16 oz) cock's combs, livers, wattles, 2 eggs, 1 egg yolk, 1 lemon, a little butter, flour, stock, salt and freshly ground pepper

Wash the livers and carefully remove the gall bladder which is extremely bitter. Cut the livers into two or three pieces. Skin the chicken's combs and wattlers in boiling water and cut them up. Put a little butter in a pan on the heat and cook the combs and wattles first for 20 minutes, then add the livers and finally eggs. Season with salt and pepper, add a glassful of stock (a cube can be used), and bring it all to cooking temperature. Separately beat two egg yolks together with a tiny bit of flour, the juice of half a lemon and a glassful of hot stock added a little at a time.

Pour this sauce on to the other mixture and cook it all together for two minutes, stirring constantly.

Braised beef

1 kg (2 1/4 pounds) beef, 2 fine onions, 1 stick celery, 2 or 3 carrots, 2 cloves garlic, 500 g (1 pound) fresh or tinned peeled tomatoes, 1 glass red wine, rosemary, basil, sage, parsley, cloves, extra virgin olive oil, salt and pepper

Finely chop the garlic and rosemary, add salt and pepper and put this mixture into little incisions specially cut in the meat. Tie up the meat and brown it in three tablespoonfuls of oil. Chop together the onion, celery, carrots, parsley, sage and a few leaves of basil, salt lightly and cook in a little oil over a moderate heat for about 20 minutes. At this stage add the glass of wine, let it evaporate, then add the cloves and the pureed tomatoes. Let it all cook for a further 20 minutes, pass it through a sieve and add it to the meat. Let it cook for three or four hours, adding a little hot stock if necessary. Carve the meat into fairly thick slices and serve it with some of the sauce in which it was cooked. Use the rest of the sauce as a dressing over the pasta.

Milk veal

800 g (1 3/4 pounds) best end of milk veal, 2 cloves garlic, 1 sprig of rosemary, 75 g (3 oz) butter, extra virgin olive oil, 3/4 litre (3 cups) milk, salt and pepper

Chop the garlic with the rosemary and spread it over the surface of the meat, which has been tied up with a colourless thread. Using a large casserole, brown the meat gently on all sides in two generous tablespoonfuls of oil and the butter. Add the hot milk, a little at a time, season with salt (and pepper if liked) cover and let it cook for about an hour. Turn the meat frequently so that it does not stick to the sides of the casserole. When it is done, keep it hot between two plates. Rub the sauce through a sieve, re-warm it and distribute it over the thinly sliced meat.

Kidneys with parsley and oil

3 small kidneys from milk veal, 50 g (2 oz) butter, a little oil, parsley, half glass of white wine, 1 tbsp. flour, salt

Open up the kidneys and remove all the fat. Cut them into rounds and then cover with boiling salted water. When the water is cold, take out the kidneys, dry them and put them into a pan for a moment to draw out all the water which must be thrown away. Flour the kidneys lightly, place them in a sieve to remove all excess flour, then put them into a frying pan with 25 g (1 oz) butter and two tablespoonfuls of oil. Season with salt and pepper, add the wine and let it evaporate quickly. One minute before removing the kidneys from the heat, add the remaining butter, the chopped parsley and, if necessary, a tablespoonful or two of stock.
The kidneys must only be cooked very briefly to stay tender.

Florentine style tripe

1200 g (2 1/2 pounds) previously boiled tripe (the round sort), 500 g (1 pounds) fresh or tinned peeled tomatoes, 1 carrot, 1 onion, 1 stick of celery, 1 glass of stock, parmesan, extra virgin olive oil, butter, salt and pepper

Cut the tripe into long thin strips and wash it in plenty of cold water. Chop the onion, carrot and celery and brown them for a few minutes in three or four tablespoonfuls of olive oil. Add the tripe and brown for a few minutes, seasoning with salt and pepper. Add the pureed tomatoes and the stock. Cover and cook for 15/20 minutes on a low heat. When the tripe is done, turn up the heat if necessary to thicken the sauce. Add a generous amount of grated parmesan, and a nut-sized piece of butter. Serve very hot, either as a first or second course.

Pork liver

800 g (1 3/4 pounds) pork liver, 300 g (12 oz) caul of pork, bay leaves, sage, fennel, extra virgin olive oil, salt and pepper

Cut the liver into egg-sized pieces, and season generously with salt and pepper. Cut the caul into squares and use these to wrap

up each piece of liver together with a fresh
bay leaf and a little sage. Fasten the caul with
a toothpick. Put the wrapped pieces of liver
into a pan with two or three tablespoonfuls
of oil, plus a small sprig of fennel and let
them brown for a few seconds. Pour in half
a glass of red wine and when this has
evaporated, add a ladleful of stock. Let it all
cook slowly so that the caul dissolves
completely.

Roast pheasant

*1 pheasant weighing approx. 1 1/2 kg (3 1/2 pounds),
150 g (6 oz) rather fatty prosciutto, 50 g (2 oz) bacon,
sage, extra virgin olive oil, salt and pepper*

Make sure that the pheasant is very well
hung, plucked and singed. Wash and dry it.
Stuff it with a mixture of minced prosciutto,
bacon, sage, salt and pepper, first putting
aside two slices of the prosciutto. Wrap these
two slices round the breast of the pheasant,
and tie it up with kitchen string. Place the
bird in a baking tin with three tablespoonfuls
of oil and put it in the oven, preheated to 180
C. Turn frequently as it cooks, and baste with
its own sauce. When the pheasant is ready,
remove the string, carve the bird, pour over
the de-greased sauce, and serve with the
stuffing.

"Uccelletti scappati" (Little meat rolls)

(600 g /1 1/2 pounds) veal in thin slices, 100 g (4 oz) prosciutto, 1 small onion, 50 g (2 oz) ham, sage, extra virgin olive oil, 1/2 glass white wine, a little stock, salt and pepper

Chop together very finely the bacon and the onion, adding salt and pepper. Place an equal-sized slice of ham on top of each slice of meat, and on top of this a small sage leaf and a pinch of the chopped bacon and onion mixture.

Roll the meat up round this filling and secure the little rolls with a toothpick. Place them in a baking tin with two or three tablespoonfuls of oil and a few more sage leaves. Put the tin in the oven, preheated to 180 C. To help the cooking process, first add half a glass of white wine and then a few tablespoonfuls of stock. Be cautious with the salt because the ham releases its own salt during cooking which also flavours the meat.

Chicken Florentine style

A local domestic chicken weighing about 1200 g (2 1/2 pounds), 25 g (1 oz) dried mushrooms, 500 g (1 pound) peeled tomatoes, 2 glasses of stock, extra virgin olive oil, 50 g (2 oz) butter, 1 small glass of white wine, flour, salt and pepper

Soften the mushrooms in a glass of lukewarm stock. Clean and singe the chicken and divide it up into 8 pieces. Put these in a pan with 30 g (1 oz) of butter and two tablespoonfuls of oil, and brown gently. Pour in the wine and let it evaporate. Add the mushrooms and the stock in which they are soaking, first passing it through a fine strainer so as not to include any earth. Add the diced tomatoes (they can be bought ready chopped in a tin), and let it all cook for 45 minutes, adding the remaining stock a little at a time. Before taking the chicken off the heat, dilute one tablespoonful of flour in 25 g (1 oz) of melted butter, and add this to the sauce to give it a creamy consistency.

Rabbit with olives

1 rabbit weighing 1200 g (2 1/2 pounds) (drawn weight), 200 g (8 oz) pureed tomatoes, 1 onion, 1 garlic clove, 1 sprig of rosemary, 100 g (4 oz) black olives, 1 glassful white wine, extra virgin olive oil, salt and pepper

Wash and dry the rabbit, and cut it into fairly small pieces. Lightly brown a chopped onion in half a glassful of oil, add the rabbit and when this has also turned colour, pour in the white wine and let it evaporate. Add two tablespoonfuls of tomato puree diluted with a little stock, season with salt and pepper, cover and cook for about an hour. Chop a small handful of spiky rosemary leaves plus a garlic clove, and add these to the rabbit together with the olives. Let the flavours mingle for a further five minutes, then serve hot accompanied by potatoes cooked with rosemary.

Sweet and sour veal

1 kg (2 1/4 pounds) veal, 1 kg (2 1/4 pounds) fresh or tinned peeled tomatoes, 2 onions, 2 sticks of celery, 2 carrots, generous amount of parsley, extra virgin olive oil, 1 glass red wine, salt and pepper

for the sauce: 100 g (4 oz) raisins, 50 g (2 oz) pine nuts, 30 g (1 oz) plain dark chocolate, 50 g (2 oz) candied citron, a pinch of powdered cinnamon, 3 cloves, 30 g (1 oz) sugar, 2 tbsp vinegar

Chop together very finely the vegetables (excluding tomatoes) and put them in a deep pan together with the meat and a glassful of olive oil, salt and pepper. Cook, uncovered, on a moderate heat for about half an hour. Add a glassful of red wine and then cover the pan. Stir from time to time, and when the wine has evaporated, add the pureed tomatoes and continue cooking, covered, for one and a half hours to thicken the sauce.

Cut the meat into slices and put it back into its sauce. Add the raisins, pinenuts, grated chocolate, candied citron, sugar, cinnamon and cloves. Sprinkle on the vinegar and cook everything together for a further 15 minutes. Serve very hot, even the following day, which is recommended

The following can also be cooked in the same way: hare, rabbit, wild boar and beef tongue.

Fried pancake strips with sauce

6 eggs, 1 tbsp. flour, 400 g (16 oz) fresh tomatoes or 200 g (8 oz) tomato puree, 1 tbsp. grated parmesan, 1 small onion, 1 small stick of celery, parsley, basil, extra virgin olive oil, 1 stock cube, milk, salt and pepper, parmesan to sprinkle

Chop together very finely the onion, celery, parsley and basil. Gently soften them in three tablespoonfuls of oil, and then add the pureed tomatoes. Season with salt and pepper, and let it all cook for 15 minutes. If the sauce it too thick, add a few spoonfuls of stock.
Meanwhile, beat the eggs in a bowl, add a heaped tablespoonful of flour, previously mixed with the milk, plus two tablespoonfuls of parmesan and a pinch of salt and pepper (optional). Blend well, and use this mixture

to make pancakes which should not be too thick.

When the pancakes are cold, cut them into strips the same size as tagliatelle pasta. Put these strips into the sauce prepared as above, and leave on a moderate heat for 10 minutes, stirring gently to mingle the flavours.

Serve hot with plenty of grated parmesan.

SIDE DISHES

Beans with oil

300 g (12 oz) cannellini beans, 1 clove garlic, 2 sage leaves, extra virgin olive oil, salt and pepper

Put the beans into an earthenware cooking pot together with cold water, pepper, a few sage leaves, a garlic clove and a tablespoonful of olive oil. Keep the pot on a very low flame, using a heat-reducing mat so that the beans do not break up during the long cooking process, which must take at least three hours. Only add salt after they are cooked. With this system, it is possible to avoid soaking the beans overnight, and the result is better. When they are ready, drain and serve them very hot, with a sprinkling of good quality extra virgin olive oil, freshly harvested if available.

"Fagioli all'uccelletto" (Beans with tomato sauce)

300 g (12 oz) cannellini beans, 2 cloves garlic, 3 sage leaves, 300 g (12 oz) pureed tomatoes, extra virgin olive oil, salt and pepper

Boil the beans as in the preceding recipe, and drain very thoroughly. Whilst they are drying, brown the garlic in two tablespoonfuls of oil, using an earthenware cooking pot. Add the

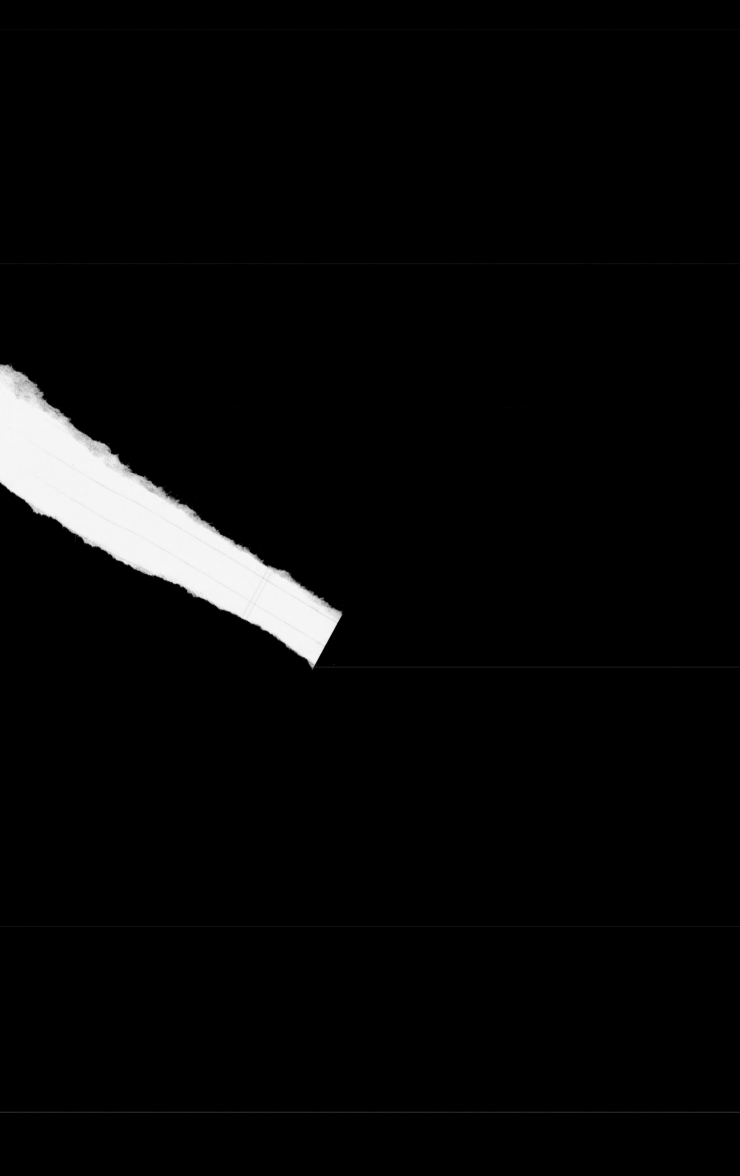

pureed tomatoes and the sage leaves. Season with salt and pepper and let it cook for 10 minutes. Put in the beans, stir carefully with a wooden spoon, and continue cooking for 10 minutes. This is an ideal accompaniment for grilled sausages or "cotechino" (boiled pork sausage).

Potatoes cooked in the oven

1 kg (2 1/4 pounds) potatoes, 3 cloves garlic, 1 sprig rosemary, extra virgin olive oil, salt and pepper

Before peeling the potatoes, boil them for a few minutes in lightly salted water, then peel and cut them into chunks (not too small). Put these potato pieces into a wide, possibly rectangular baking tin, together with four tablespoonfuls of oil, the roughly chopped garlic cloves, the rosemary, salt and pepper. Roast the potatoes in the oven at 180 C until they are deep golden brown. (It will take nearly two hours).

This in the old fashioned recipe for roast potatoes, placed in a dripping pan under the meat which turned as it cooked in the oven. The sauce formed during the roasting process would slowly drip on to the potatoes, imparting the goodness and the flavour of the revolving meat. Only one change has been made: the potatoes are parboiled to save cooking time and give a more uniform result.

Florentine style peas

1200 g (2 1/2 pounds) fresh peas (to be shelled), 50 g (2 oz) ham, 50 g (2 oz) bacon, parsley, sugar, extra virgin olive oil, salt

Choose very small peas, shell and wash them. Put two tablespoonfuls of oil in an earthenware casserole and for just a few second fry the ham and bacon, cut into thin strips, plus the garlic, whole (so that it can possibly be removed later). Add the peas, the chopped parsley and a fraction of a spoonful of sugar. Cover it all with cold water. Simmer the peas very gently for about half an hour, and salt them moderately before taking them off the heat. Serve hot, with a little of their cooking water.

"Cardi" Florentine style (cardoon)

1 kg cardi (2 1/4 pounds) 100 g (4 oz) butter, 1 lemon, 1/4 litre (1 cup) milk, 1 tbsp. flour, salt

Clean the cardi, removing the leaves, the core and the damaged and stringy parts. Cut the cardi into pieces, 8/10 cm long, and wash them in the water acidulated with plenty of lemon juice. Boil in salted water containing a tablespoonful of flour, which keep the cardi white. When these are cooked, drain and dry them on a clean linen cloth. If necessary, remove any remaining stringy bits. Flour the cardi pieces lightly and fry them in butter, being careful the butter does not burn. Put them one after another, as they are ready, in a buttered fireproof dish. Season with salt, cover with milk and put them in the oven, preheated to 180-200C. Leave in the oven until the milk has been cooked to a creamy consistency, and is lightly brown on top. (The butter and flour used to fry the cardi, together with the milk give "body" to the final cream).

Baked spinach and carrot mould

1 kg (2 1/4 pounds) spinach, 1 kg (2 1/4 pounds) carrots, 100 g (4 oz) butter, 50 g (2 oz) flour, 1 litre (4 cups) milk, 4 eggs, nutmeg, parmesan, breadcrumbs, salt and pepper

Wash the spinach very thoroughly, then cook it with just the water which stays on the leaves after washing. Salt moderately. Scrape and wash the carrots, then either boil them, or possibly steam them. Rub the carrots and the spinach through a sieve – each separately

– then sauté them, also separately, in a frying pan, with a nut-size piece of butter. Afterwards put them into two different bowls. To each separate bowl add a whole egg plus an extra yolk, a handful of grated parmesan and a pinch of nutmeg. Season with salt and pepper, and blend well.

Prepare a bechamel sauce using 60 g (2 or 3 oz) butter, 50 g (2 oz) of flour, and sufficient milk to make a smooth but fairly thick sauce. Divide this sauce between the two bowls, and stir to blend it in well.

Butter a ring-shaped pudding mould and shake breadcrumbs all around, removing any excess crumbs. Put in first the carrot mixture and then the spinach one. Level it off, sprinkle with breadcrumbs, and put the mould to cook in the oven, in a bain-marie, for an hour. Test with a toothpick to see if it has cooked enough.

Fried pumpkin flowers

400 g (16 oz) fresh pumpkin flowers, 100 g (4 oz) flour, extra virgin olive oil, salt

Remove the pistils and then quickly wash the flowers in cold water. Make a batter with the flour, a pinch of salt and 2 tablespoonfuls of oil. Let it rest for at least 2 hours.

Shortly before serving them, dip the flowers into the batter, and deep fry them in boiling oil. Turn them round quickly and take them out with a perforated spoon, arranging them on a tray covered with a paper serviette.
The addition of oil makes the batter crisp and very tasty.

Mushrooms with oil, tomato and herbs

1 kg (about 2 pounds) mushrooms (porcini type), 200 g (8 oz) pureed tomatoes, 2 cloves garlic, a sprig of calamint, extra virgin olive oil, salt and pepper

Carefully clean off all the earth from the mushrooms to avoid having to wash them, or rinse very quickly. Cut them into little pieces. Put two tablespoonfuls of oil into an earthenware casserole, and brown the mushrooms, the whole garlic, and the calamint. When the garlic has turned colour, add the mushrooms, season with salt and pepper, and cook it all for about 15 minutes. As soon as the mushrooms turn brown, add the pureed tomatoes and cook for a further 15/20 minutes.

DESSERTS

"Schiacciata" with grapes

1 kg (2 pounds approx.) black grapes, 500 g (1 pound)
bread dough, 150 g (6 oz) sugar, extra virgin olive oil, salt

Knead the dough together with 4
tablespoonfuls of oil, 50 g (2 oz) sugar and
a pinch of salt. Roll half of it out thinly into
a rectangular shape the same size as the
baking tin. Grease the tin and line it with the
thinly rolled out dough. Sprinkle this with
four tablespoonfuls of sugar and half of the
grapes, previously washed and dried. Roll out
the remaining dough, and put this on top to
form a second layer. Sprinkle with the rest
of the grapes. Let it rise in a warm place, then
sprinkle with sugar and cook it for half an
hour at 180/200 C.

Rice fritters

1/2 litre (2 cups) milk, 100 g (4 oz) rice, 50 g (2 oz)
flour, 50 g (2 oz) raisins, 3 eggs, butter, sugar, rum,
lemon peel, 1 packet baking powder, extra virgin olive
oil, salt

Cook the rice in the milk, with a pinch of salt,
until it has nearly disintegrated. Add boiling
milk if it gets too dry (at the end the rice
should be dry, but soft). Remove from the
heat and let it cool until lukewarm, then add

the eggs, one at a time, plus the flour mixed with the baking powder, the raisins, previously softened in lukewarm water then dried, and a tablespoonful of rum. Let the mixture rest in a warm place.

Heat up some olive oil in a frying pan, and when it is very hot but not boiling, drop in the mixture by the spoonful to make little fritters which will puff up immediately. Turn them over, and as soon as they are a golden colour on both sides, take them out of the pan using a perforated spoon. Put them on to absorbent kitchen paper.

Serve hot, sprinkled with sugar.

Florentine "Schiacciata"

2 eggs, 7 tbsp. sugar, 10 tbsp. flour, 4 tbsp. extra virgin olive oil, 7 tbsp. milk, 1 orange, 1 scant packet of baking powder, icing sugar

Work well together the eggs and sugar, and in the following order add: oil, milk, grated orange rind, strained orange juice and flour. Mix again, then add the baking powder, blending it in well.

Butter a wide, shallow baking tin, put the mixture into it, and bake for 20/25 minutes at 200 C. When the "schiacciata" has cooled to lukewarm, take it out of the tin and sprinkle it with icing sugar.

Portuguese milk

6 eggs, 1 litre (4 cups) milk, 100 g (4 oz) sugar, 1 lemon

Put the milk on to boil with the lemon peel and reduce it to 3/4 litre (3 cups). Let it cool. Meantime, beat the whole eggs with the sugar and pour on the strained milk. Stir well to blend.
Caramelise a pudding basin with 200 g (8 oz) sugar and a tablespoon of lemon juice. Turn the basin around so that the caramel covers the whole surface. Pour the egg and milk mixture into the basin, put this into a bain-marie containing pre-heated water, and cook in the oven at 180 C for about 45 minutes. Use a toothpick to test whether the pudding has finished cooking - The toothpick should come out dry after it has been stuck in the pudding.

"Cenci" (Fried cookies)

300 g (12 oz) flour, 2 eggs, 2 tbsp. sugar, 1 glass of "vinsanto" wine, 1 lemon, salt, powdered sugar for sprinkling

Put the following ingredients on to a pastry board and take time to work them well together: flour. eggs, softened butter, sugar, grated lemon rind, a pinch of salt, and the wine. After this, wrap the dough in a linen cloth and put it in a cool place to rest for an hour.

Roll the dough out thinly and, using a notched pastry wheel, cut it into strips (which will spiral as soon as they are put into the oil). Deep fry in very hot oil, and put them on absorbent paper afterwards to dry off excess frying oil.

Put the cookies into a large bowl, sprinkling with sugar as they are ready.

"Zuccotto" (Frozen cream cake)

300 g (12 oz) sponge cake, 50 g (2 oz) plain chocolate, 50 g (2 oz) chocolate flakes, 50 g (2 oz) icing sugar, 30 g (1 oz) peeled almonds, 50 g (2 oz) candied citron and orange, 500 g (1 pound) fresh cream, 1 small glass Cointreau

Cut the sponge cake horizontally into slices and use these to line a round, smooth pudding basin.

Lightly moisten the slices with the liqueur. Whip the cream together with the icing sugar and add the ground almonds, the chocolate flakes, and the tiny pieces of candied fruit (which can be bought already cut up). Divide the mixture into two parts.

Add the melted chocolate to one part. Tip the

white mixture first into the pudding basin, and make it stick to the sponge cake lining the sides. Leave a space in the middle and fill this with the chocolate mixture. Keep it in the freezer for at least three hours before serving.

INDEX

64

«Traditional Italian Recipes»